STEAM, SMOKE, AND STEEL

Back in Time with Trains

Patrick O'Brien

Charlesbridge

When I grow up, I want to drive a train,
just like my dad does.

I think my dad's got the best job in the world. He's an engineer. Up in the cab of his giant locomotive he controls ten thousand tons of rolling steel. Coal, oil, lumber, cars—whatever needs to be carried by rail, he hauls it with his 4,400-horsepower diesel engine. One day I counted more than a hundred freight cars lined up behind his engine. That train was more than a mile long!

Have you ever noticed that there's usually more than one engine pulling a train? When the locomotives are joined up like that, it's called a consist. The engines working together can pull really heavy loads. My dad controls all the engines in his consist from his seat in the front of the first locomotive.

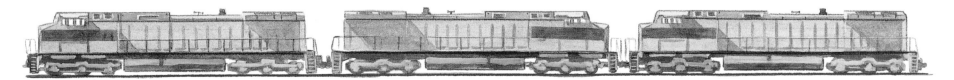

These three engines make a consist.

Computer controls in the cab help drive the train, but my dad does a lot of the driving with hand controls. To start the train, my father releases the brake and moves the reverser to the "Forward" setting. Then he uses the throttle to set the speed. The throttle has eight speeds, from "Run 1" up to "Run 8." He begins slowly at "Run 1," and when he gets to "Run 8" he's going seventy miles per hour. His train thunders down the tracks, like my grandfather's train did thirty years before.

When my dad was a kid in the 1960s, he sometimes got to ride on *his* dad's train.

My grandfather's locomotive was smaller and had less
pulling power than my dad's, but it worked the same way.
The diesel engines turned electric generators. The generators
made electricity, and the electricity turned the wheels
to make the train go. That's why diesel locomotives are
sometimes called diesel-electric locomotives.

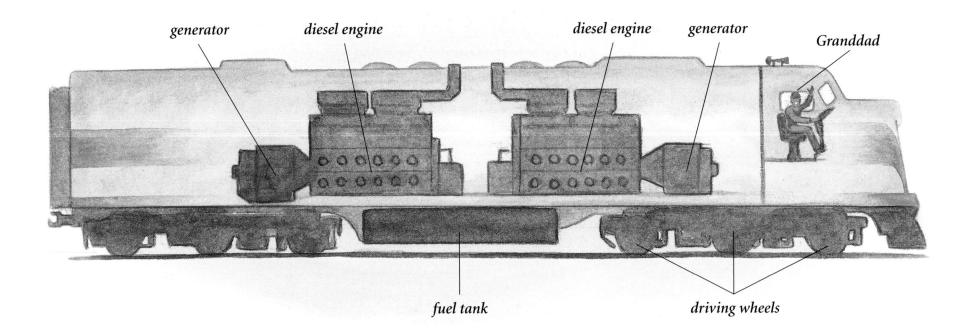

generator

diesel engine

diesel engine

generator

Granddad

fuel tank

driving wheels

My dad loves to tell me stories about riding with his father in the cab of that old diesel. "I'll never forget the time," he'll say, "when my dad let me ride with him all the way up from Florida. We were hauling a circus train. You should have seen it when we stopped in those little towns along the way. The elephants were let out and your granddaddy and I took them for a walk down the street. The clowns and acrobats would come out and start doing a show just for the fun of it. I tell you, those folks in those towns had never seen anything like it!"

But my grandfather tells different stories. When he was still a kid, trains ran on steam power instead of diesel. The locomotives were like great big smoking, puffing monsters. My grandfather says he always wanted to drive one of those old steam locomotives, like his mom did back in the old days.

It was very unusual to find a woman engineer in the 1930s, but they say my great-grandmother was an unusual woman. My grandfather still remembers the puffing smoke, hissing steam, and his mom smiling and waving as her train pulled in to the station.

My great-grandmother drove a steam locomotive. The diesel-electric locomotive had just been invented, but she didn't like the brand-new diesels that she began seeing around the train yard. Yes, they were shiny and modern, but she was a romantic. She loved the billowing steam and smoke, the big driving wheels, and the red-hot firebox of her big old steam engine. Somehow those new diesels just didn't have as much charm as the classic steamers.

The old steam engines were not as efficient as the newer diesels, though. A steam engine had to stop about every hundred miles to fill up on coal and water. It made a lot of thick, black smoke that clogged up the air in the cities, and it was also really noisy. A diesel did not have to stop as often to fill up on fuel, and it was quieter and cleaner than a steam engine. From the 1930s to the 1950s, almost all the railroads in the country replaced their old steam locomotives with diesels.

A lot of locomotives from my great-grandmother's time were designed with smooth curves and flowing lines. This was called streamlining, and it was supposed to make the train look faster and more modern. Some people said that the streamliners looked like they were going fast even when they were standing still. There were lots of different streamliners. Some were diesel, and some were steam. Underneath the smooth surfaces, though, my great-grandmother's locomotive was a lot like the one that her father had driven years before.

The M-10000 was the first streamliner. It was a diesel.

This streamliner, the Twentieth Century Limited, traveled between New York and Chicago in just sixteen hours.

Some people said this kind of streamliner looked like an upside-down bathtub.

This was called the "shark-nosed" engine.

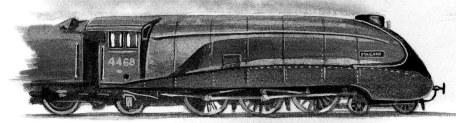

This was a British streamliner called "The Mallard."

My great-great-grandfather drove a train in the 1900s. When his daughter first saw that train, she knew just what she wanted to do when she grew up. She wanted to be an engineer and drive a train like her dad.

My great-great-grandfather started working on trains as a fireman. A fireman on a train didn't put out a fire—he kept it going. He rode in the cab with the engineer and shoveled coal from the tender into the fire in the firebox. In a steam engine, coal or wood was burned in the firebox to heat the water in the huge boiler. This made lots and lots of steam, and the steam was used as power to make the train run.

smoke

boiler
The boiler was filled with water.

firebox

coal

steam

water

tender
The tender car was right behind the engine. It carried the coal and water that the locomotive needed to run.

A fireman's job was tough, hot, and dirty. He had to keep the fire burning at just the right heat. He also had to keep up a steady pace with his shoveling—if he slowed down, so did the train.

In his years as a fireman, my great-great-grandfather shoveled tons and tons of coal. Somehow he found time to keep an eye on the engineer beside him, and he learned how to drive the mighty locomotive. Finally he became an engineer, just like his father had been years before.

My great-great-grandfather grew up in the days
of the classic American-type steam locomotive.
His dad, my great-great-great-grandfather,
drove one in the 1870s.

This is an American-type locomotive. This train was built for crossing the wide-open spaces of the young United States.

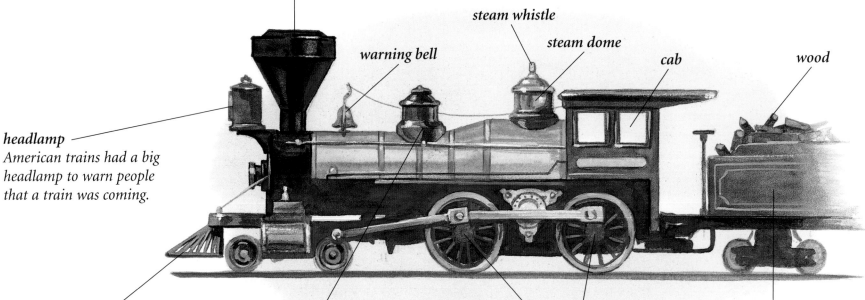

balloon smokestack
Early American trains burned wood instead of coal because there was so much forestland in the U.S. Burning embers shoot up from a fire made with wood, so the stack had to be made tall and wide to catch them.

steam whistle

steam dome

warning bell

cab

wood

headlamp
American trains had a big headlamp to warn people that a train was coming.

tender

cowcatcher
America was a big country, and railroad tracks were laid out over miles and miles of open land with no fences. Sometimes animals wandered onto the tracks. The cowcatcher cleared the tracks of animals or anything else.

sandbox
On days when the rails were slippery, sand from the sandbox was fed by a tube to the rail just in front of the driving wheels. This gave the wheels more grip.

driving wheels
These were the only wheels turned by the engine.

My great-great-great-grandfather liked to tell stories, too. His favorite was about the time his train was held up by the famous outlaw Jesse James. James and his gang had piled a bunch of logs on the tracks to force the train to stop. The bandits had their six-shooters out, and they made the passengers get out of the train and hand over all their money. Everyone was really scared, but my great-great-great-grandfather made sure that no one got hurt.

In those days there were several brakemen on the train. There was no brake for the whole train—each car had its own. When the train needed to stop or slow down, the brakemen had to run along the tops of the cars and turn the wheel of the handbrake on each car. This was a very dangerous job, especially on cold, snowy days. But in the late 1870s, an airbrake was developed so that the engineer could stop the train by himself with a lever up in his cab.

My great-great-great-great-grandfather drove a
train in the 1850s, in the early days of railroads.
The ride was slow and bumpy, but his son
loved to go along anytime he could.

Railroad companies were being started all along the east coast of the United States in the 1850s. The railroads laid tracks between the big cities in the east and began spreading west toward the Ohio and Mississippi Rivers.

It wasn't easy to lay out a railroad, especially over land with lots of rivers, hills, and mountains. A train can't go up a steep hill, and it can't go around a sharp curve, so the tracks had to be made as flat and straight as possible. The railroad workers built bridges over valleys and drilled tunnels through mountains. It took a lot of time and money, but it was worth it. With the railroads in place, people could travel a lot faster and a lot farther, and things like coal, cattle, and other heavy stuff could be shipped over long distances. My great-great-great-great-grandfather was proud to be a part of it, since his father had helped to get it all started.

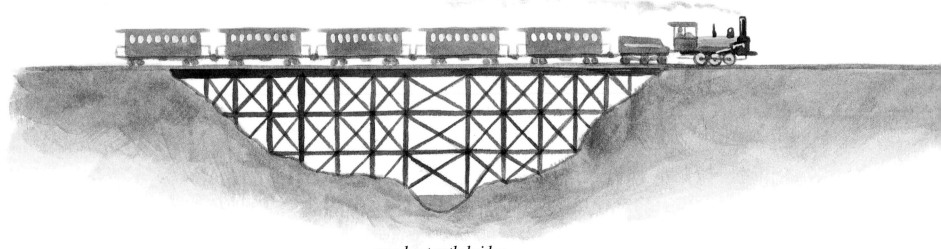

wooden trestle bridge

Sometimes it was easier to cut a big trench through a hill than to tunnel through it.

Workers built these early tunnels with hand tools like shovels and picks. But they had a little help—they used dynamite for blasting rock away.

In the 1830s, my great-great-great-great-grandfather
sometimes rode along with his dad on one of the
first trains in the United States.

My great-great-great-great-great-grandfather liked to brag that he was one of the very first people ever to drive a train in this country. Before trains, people traveled in stagecoaches and buggies. People had never traveled faster than the speed of a running horse, and at first they weren't too sure about this brand-new invention called a steam locomotive.

One time my great-great-great-great-great-great-grandfather decided to prove that his machine could go faster and pull more weight than a horse ever could. He set up a race: his locomotive, pulling three cars and twenty people, against a horse and carriage with three people inside. He gave the horse a small head start and then set off down the rails.

Smoke came pouring out of the smokestack of the little engine, and the passengers were choked with black smoke and showered with burning embers. Ladies put up their umbrellas for protection but then had to throw them out the windows when they started to catch on fire. People were amazed that the train could actually go almost twenty miles per hour!

After ten miles the train crossed the finish line a mile ahead of the horse. The horse was all tired out, but the locomotive was puffing away, ready to go another ten miles. The passengers' clothes were ruined by the rain of sparks, but they could all see that trains were the way of the future.

So I guess you could say that trains run in my family.
My father, my grandfather, my great-grandmother, my
great-great . . . well, you get the idea—they all drove
trains. When I'm a grown-up, I want to drive a train, too.
And maybe then I'll have a kid of my own. . . .

For Eamon, who likes wheels
—P. O'B.

Published by Charlesbridge
85 Main Street, Watertown, MA 02472
(617) 926-0329
www.charlesbridge.com

Library of Congress Cataloging-in-Publication Data
O'Brien, Patrick, 1960–
Steam, smoke, and steel: back in time with trains/Patrick O'Brien.
p. cm.
Summary: A boy traces the development of railroad engines from coal to steam
to diesel as he recounts his family's experience of driving trains over the years.
ISBN-13: 978-0-88106-969-3; ISBN-10: 0-88106-969-8 (reinforced for library use)
ISBN-13: 978-0-88106-972-3; ISBN-10: 0-88106-972-8 (softcover)
1. Locomotives—Juvenile literature. 2. Railroads—Trains—Juvenile literature.
[1. Locomotives. 2. Railroads—Trains.] I. Title.
TJ605.5.O27 2000
385'.36—dc21 99-053968

Printed in Korea
(hc) 10 9 8 7 6 5 4 3
(sc) 10 9 8 7 6 5 4 3

Illustrations done in watercolor and gouache on watercolor paper
Display type and text type set in Greco and Minion
Color separations made by Eastern Rainbow, Derry, New Hampshire
Printed and bound by Sung In Printing, South Korea
Production supervision by Brian G. Walker
Designed by Diane M. Earley